Magadh

Magadh

Shrikant Verma

*Translated from the Hindi
by Rahul Soni*

&

SHEFFIELD – LONDON – NEW YORK

First published in the UK in 2025 by And Other Stories
Sheffield – London – New York
www.andotherstories.org

Originally published in Hindi as *Magadh* in 1984.

First published in Rahul Soni's English in India by Almost Island Books in 201
This revised translation first published by Eka, an imprint of Westland Books, In

1 3 5 7 9 8 6 4 2

ISBN: 9781916751330
eBook ISBN: 9781916751347

Proofreader: Alex Middleton; Typesetter: Tetragon, London; Typefaces:
Albertan Pro and Linotype Syntax (interior) and Stellage (cover); Series
Cover Design: Elisa von Randow, Alles Blau Studio, Brazil, after a concept
by And Other Stories; Author Photo: © Shrikant Verma Trust.

Grateful acknowledgement is made to the following, in which
some of these translations first appeared: *Almost Island*, *Asymptote*,
PN Review, *The Poetry Review*, *Sheffield Telegraph* and the *TLS*.

And Other Stories books are printed and bound in the UK on FSC-
certified paper by the CPI Group (UK) Ltd, Croydon.

A catalogue record for this book is available from the British Library.

And Other Stories' Authorized Representative within the EU
GPSR legal framework is: Logos Europe, 9 rue Nicolas Poussin,
17000 La Rochelle, France. E-mail: Contact@logoseurope.eu

And Other Stories gratefully acknowledge that our work is
supported using public funding by Arts Council England.

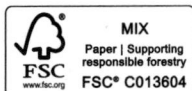

Supported using public funding by
**ARTS COUNCIL
ENGLAND**

MIX
Paper | Supporting
responsible forestry
FSC® C013604

For Nirmal Verma

CONTENTS

TRANSLATOR'S NOTE

first encountered Shrikant Verma's *Magadh* in 2007. A friend
ad recommended it to me, and I started translating it almost
immediately, before I had even finished reading the collection
. its entirety.

The first edition of this translation came out in 2013, and it
a curious feeling, revisiting these poems more than a decade
ter.

I remember, when I first read them, being struck most of all
y the language, which is, I think, still the most arresting thing
oout the collection – the almost-paradox of its pared-down
ocabulary and repetitions, against the slippery circularity
ad riddle-like ambiguities of its locutions. There was also
e intense, often unbearably overwhelming, even indiscrim-
ate, sense of loss – for times, for places, for people – that
aunted its pages. I had never translated anything until then;
. fact, I didn't think of what I had begun doing as 'translation'
all – I was just so struck by the voice of these poems that
wanted to see if it was possible to achieve those effects in
e language I wrote in, i.e., English.

In the years since, I have seen these poems become more and
ore relevant and urgent, speaking with what might seem like

remarkable prescience and precision about our current politic
moment. Except that they were actually a response to a simil
moment almost fifty years ago. (Although they are also, li⟩
any great work of art, much more than just a response to o⟩
particular moment in time.) I also discovered that the langua⟩
employed in *Magadh* and the feeling that suffuses these poen⟩
are something of an anomaly even in Verma's oeuvre. Whi⟩
perhaps gives one a sense of how immediate and visceral the
poems must have felt when they were first written (some
1979, and the bulk of them in 1984) and when they were fir⟩
published in Hindi. These are no mere abstractions.

And now the wheel of history has come full circle – and hc⟩
quickly, and with no lessons learnt.

*

The first few poems launch us straight into the world ⟨
the book – by and large set around the historical empire ⟨
Magadh, during the period (roughly the sixth to the secor⟩
century BCE) when it grew, under rulers such as Bimbisar⟩
Ajatashatru, Chandragupta and Ashoka, from a powerf⟩
kingdom in the eastern part of the Indian subcontinent to o⟩
of the greatest empires the world had seen, with Pataliputr⟩
once a minor fortress town, becoming its capital and turnir⟩
into one of the world's major urban centres.

And then, it all fell into decadence and decline.

But there is
neither Magadh nor Magadh
You too have been searching

brothers,
this is not the Magadh
you've read about
in books,
this is the Magadh
that you
like me
have lost

round it and after it, various other kingdoms (Avanti, Kosal, Videha, etc.), cities (Hastinapur, Kashi, Kosambi, Nalanda, Takshashila, Ujjaini, etc.) and dynasties (the Guptas, the Licchavis, etc.) of antiquity, too, went through their own life cycles, as did religions and schools of thought and art.

These are not just historical people and places, however — most of them have a rich existence in mythology, in classical and religious literature, in the imagination of a people and their culture. The resonances run vast and deep. And one of the most interesting things Verma does is to overlay the historical with the mythic and the literary — his allusions range from the *Ramayana*, the *Mahabharata* and the Puranas to Buddhist texts, from the *Kathasaritsagara* to the plays of Bhasa and Bhavabhuti — magnifying in almost subliminal ways the reach of these poems into the recesses of the readers' psyches.

That being said, I have always held that a knowledge of the places mentioned in *Magadh* is not necessary for an understanding of the poems. They function more as totems of a sort — a vague idea of them as cities and kingdoms that existed once, were once powerful, and are now no more, lie almost forgotten, is what haunts the poems. And I think that a more detailed knowledge – or seeking to understand the poems in terms c specifics with respect to the places and names mentioned might even distract from getting to what they are trying to sa They are meant to throw a shadow, and perhaps *only* a shadov

The 'pastness' of *Magadh*, at least in my reading of it, is not pastness that is rooted in the specifics of history, in its detail but more in the idea of history being cyclical, of the essenti; nature of things (i.e., people, kingdoms, civilisations, powe remaining the same, the fact that there are discernible patterr which will repeat themselves, and the weariness, the sense c resignation and futility that such a realisation engenders. (An indeed, the realisation of the futility of art in the face of th; inexorable turning: 'What I wrote, useless / What I did no / meaningless'.)

If there is a movement within this cyclical pattern of his tory, perhaps we see it in how the collection itself moves fro mourning, to resisting and searching, to some sort of unde standing and acceptance. But in the end, we die, what was lo; stays lost, and we start all over again, having learnt nothin really, forever doomed to repeat ourselves.

The only consolation, if there's any consolation to be ha is that, perhaps, in the larger scheme of things, whatever th; may be, none of this matters at all. It is only fitting, then, th; the last word in the collection goes to Time:

> I
> am old now
> I write
> my name
> in chalk

on every blank wall
I come across

The next day I find
someone has rubbed it out
so thoroughly
as if it had never been written

Now when I shout –
Who did this?
I get the answer –
Time

ime, it must be noted, comes up in the very first poem too,
the voice of a vetal – a malevolent spirit that possesses and
animates corpses.

recognise me?
Vetal –
my deeds
left me hanging
from a diseased branch
of the tree
        of Time

he most famous vetal of all is, of course, the one from the
ikram–Vetal tales – the riddling ghoul hanging off the back
 the great king of legend, Vikramaditya, tossing out conun-
rum after conundrum, dooming the king to repeat the same
ek through the cremation grounds over and over.

This is a very potent symbol, and a great voice – inviting y
dangerous, obsequious yet poisonous, sweet yet curdled –
lure the reader into the book and into the ideas of recurren
and futility it circles around. And to me, the form and th
language of the poems are the perfect vehicle for this idea
vision of history.

In my translations, therefore, my attempt has been to retai
the rhythms and repetitions of the original without losing i
spoken, dialogic quality. To come up with an English that ca
carry these notes naturally, without sounding antiquated
too contemporary. To mirror its simple, crystalline vocabular
To find other devices to replace or replicate the effects of th
extensive rhyming in the original. To preserve its ambiguiti
and circularities.

My method was to first try and create poems in English o
of the words and images of the originals, and then, throughou
the process of revision and editing, find my way back, step b
step, to the source. This is a process that helped me, I woul
like to think, approximate what A. K. Ramanujan and Davi
Shulman have called the 'literal force' of the text.

One of the more difficult decisions had to do with Verma
idiosyncratic punctuation. In the end, I decided to retain
for the most part, changing things only when they became to
confusing in English. A related problem was that of capita
isation: Hindi doesn't have upper- and lower-case letters, b
English does. Here, I have capitalised the first letter whereve
according to my reading, a new sentence begins, whether or n
the punctuation indicates it.

The spellings of proper names do not always follow accepte
English norms, but are a balance between what might see

atural to a Hindi speaker and what a non-Hindi reader would
ill be able to recognise or look up.

Some words have been retained from the original: maharaj,
r king; rajasuya, for a ritual that proclaims a king an emperor;
kshauhini, for a battle formation consisting of fixed numbers
f chariots, cavalry and infantry soldiers; Mahakaal, a name of
ıe god Shiva, referring to his status as the lord of time and
eath; ghat, for a series of steps leading down to a body of water,
articularly a holy river, often used for religious rites, some
ɔecifically for cremation; dom, for a member of an 'untouch-
ɔle' caste that traditionally worked as scavengers or tended to
·emation ghats. Manikarnika is the primary cremation ghat in
ashi (Varanasi), on the banks of the river Ganga, and is con-
dered especially sacred. Ambapali and Amrapali both refer
· the famous courtesan of Ujjaini – Verma uses both forms
֧ the name, and I have as well.

Revisiting these translations revealed a number of instances,
ıg and small, where I had strayed too far – some where
had simply misread, some where I was perhaps too enam-
ured of a formulation or word choice to let it go, some
here knowing more about the context shifted the meaning
ightly. I'm glad I had the opportunity to rectify them in this
ew edition.

In the end, I think it only appropriate to leave readers with
erma's own words about *Magadh*:

Avanti, Malwa, Ujjaini, Kshipra, Champa, Kashi,
Kosambi, Kapilavastu, Kosal, Kalinga, Vaishali, Amrapali,
Vasavadatta, Vasantasena, Chandragupta, Bimbisara, Ashoka,
Ajatashatru – a procession of characters, of protagonists, of

cities, of memories, a crowd that has gathered. That is what my poems are. Their main themes are death, destruction and moral corruption. I know what *Magadh* is – Time beyond time!

RAHUL SON

Jodhpur and Bangalore, December 20

Magadh

INVOCATION

Great benefactor! Sea of virtue! Sea of wisdom!
After many, many years
I've come to your door —

listen my host,
I bring you
stories that span generations
the sorrows of cities, of citizens —

recognise me?
Vetal —
my deeds
left me hanging
from a diseased branch
of the tree
            of Time

Great benefactor! Sea of virtue! Sea of wisdom!
By your grace
I'm born
            a human again

And now I ask you to grant me this
if I cannot give voice to you
then you
            give me voice

                                        (1984)

MAGADH

Listen horseman, where's Magadh?
I've come
from Magadh
I must go to
Magadh

Where
do I turn?
North or south,
east or west?

Here I see Magadh,
here it disappears —

just yesterday
I left Magadh
just yesterday
Magadh's people
told me not to
leave Magadh
I gave my word —
I'd be back
before sunrise

But there is
neither Magadh nor Magadh
You too have been searching

brothers,
this is not the Magadh
you've read about
in books,
this is the Magadh
that you
like me
have lost

(1979)

THE PEOPLE OF MAGADH

The people of Magadh
are sorting the bones of the dead

Which ones are Ashoka's?
And Chandragupta's?
No, no,
these can't be Bimbisara's
they are Ajatashatru's,

the people of Magadh say
and shed
tears

It's natural

those who've seen a man alive
only they
will see him dead
those who haven't seen the living
how can they see the dead?

Just yesterday
the people of Magadh
saw Ashoka
going to Kalinga
returning from Kalinga
Chandragupta riding his horse to Takshashila

Bimbisara
in tears
Ajatashatru
flexing his muscles

The people of Magadh
had seen
and they
can't forget
that they
had seen

those who
can no longer
be found

(1984)

CORPSES IN KASHI

Have you seen Kashi?
Where
corpses come and
corpses go
by the same road.

And what of corpses?
Corpses will come,
corpses will go –

ask then, Whose corpse is this?
Rohitashva's?
No, no,
all corpses can't be Rohitashva

His corpse
you'll recognise from a distance
and if not from a distance, then
from up close –
and if not from up close,
then it
can't be Rohitashva

and even if it is
will it make a difference?

Friends,
you have seen Kashi,
where
corpses come and
corpses go
by the same road.

And this is all you did –
made way
and asked –
Whose corpse is this?

Whoever it was,
whoever it wasn't,
did it make a difference?

(1984)

JUSTICE IN KASHI

The council has been dismissed
Councillors, let's go

What had to happen happened
Why then the long faces?
Why this anxiety?
What are we afraid of?

We did not judge –
merely nodding in agreement is not judgement
We didn't even give it a moment's thought

The debaters debated
what did we do?

What's our fault?
We don't call the council
We don't judge
We come to Kashi
once a year
to say only this
The council is unnecessary
everyone has already been judged
before they are born

(198.

KOSAMBI

Vasavadatta asks,
What came
before
Kosambi?

Vasavadatta!

Before Kosambi
there was only
Kosambi,

after Kosambi
there is only
Kosambi

In return for
Kosambi
you can get
only Kosambi
Searching for Kosambi
Vasavadatta
has reached
Kosambi

(1979)

HASTINAPUR

Consider
a person
who comes to Hastinapur
and says
No, no, this can't be Hastinapur!

Consider
a person
left all alone –
why should he care when the Mahabharata was fought

If you can,
consider
Hastinapur,
for which
time and again
a Mahabharata is fought,
and no one cares
except that person
who comes to Hastinapur
and says,
No, no, this can't be Hastinapur!

(198

THE CUSTOMS OF HASTINAPUR

I say again
without dharma, there can be nothing –
but no one
listens to me.
It isn't the custom to listen in Hastinapur –

those who hear
are either deaf
or have been appointed
to turn a deaf ear

I say again
without dharma, there can be nothing –
but no one
listens to me

Listen or not then
people of Hastinapur! Beware!
In Hastinapur
your enemy is being raised: Thought –
and remember
these days it spreads like the plague:
Thought.

(1984)

KAPILAVASTU

Days in Kapilavastu make the eyes sore
nights
are drowned in wine and whores

The old, cast out for being old
stop
at the border
and look back at Kapilavastu
with greedy eyes

Young brides sometimes
wake up
startled from their dreams

No one is old in Kapilavastu
there's only
the fear of being old
Being young
means only this
that no one old should be in Kapilavastu

Kapilavastu hasn't been
around
too long

(197

KAPILAVASTU CALLING

Maharaj! Let's go back –
this desire to rule over Ujjaini is,
if you ask me,
absurd –

Ujjaini is
Ujjaini no more –
neither is justice served
nor injustice

Just as
Magadh is
Magadh no more –
everyone is well fed
no longer
skin and bone

There is pity in no one
There is shame
in no one
No one thinks,
those who think once
don't think again.

It's the same in Kashi –
in Kashi
they're busy counting corpses

No one
has time for the living,
those who do can't tell
the difference between the living and the dead.

Or take Mithila –
where Videha ruled
till just yesterday
In the same Mithila
now suspicion rules
No one respects dharma –
Vishvamitra, Vasishtha,
no one remains –
Maharaj! Everyone dies
no one is immortal.

If you must go somewhere, go to Kapilavastu.
He who goes to Kapilavastu
doesn't come back
He who doesn't go to Kapilavastu
spends his life
calling out Kapilavastu! Kapilavastu!

(198

TAKSHASHILA

Soldiers seen in Takshashila
in ones and twos
Who are they looking for
Why do they seem so lost

Why do they go
to the fort
and come back
in ones and twos

bewildered
by the fact
that nothing
remains

except a pile of rubble
that every now and then
shouts
Who
created me

(1979)

UJJAINI

The courtesan
whom Kalidasa loved
filled
Ujjaini
like musk
An auspicious
concurrence
Ujjaini
Kalidasa
musk

sometimes
the stars
are so aligned

Now who comes
looking
asking
Mahakaal himself –
Is this
her city,
she
who was
everywhere
like musk

The courtesan
whom Kalidasa
loved
has she
passed by
this road

Wait, stop,
whose
corpse
is this
floating
by
on
the Kshipra

(1979)

THE ROAD TO UJJAINI

All travellers going to Ujjaini:
this road does not go to Ujjaini
and this same road goes to Ujjaini

Till yesterday I'd show the way
saying
Attention! This road goes to Ujjaini
I show the way today as well
saying
Attention! This road does not go to Ujjaini

Travellers!
The truth is that
every road goes to Ujjaini
and that
no road goes to Ujjaini

Ujjaini
forever looks to the road
Ujjaini
has turned away from roads

Then
where should those going to Ujjaini go?
They should go to Ujjaini
and say,
This is not Ujjaini

because we
did not arrive here on the roads
that go to Ujjaini
or on the roads
that don't go to Ujjaini

(1984)

NAMELESS IN AVANTI

Will it make a difference
if I say
I'm not from Magadh
I'm from Avanti?

Of course it will
you'll be taken to belong to Avanti
you'll have to forget Magadh

And you
will not be able to forget Magadh
you'll live your life
in Avanti
without knowing Avanti

Then you'll say
I'm not from Avanti
I'm from Magadh
and no one will believe you
You'll cry —
'It's true
I'm from Magadh
I'm not from Avanti'
and it will make no difference

No one will believe you are
from Magadh
No one will recognise you
in Avanti

(1984)

FICTION

Sir, hear me out
before you go
The Pataliputra
you and I
are fighting for
is in the eyes of others
a fiction

Do you hear?

For them it's not worth
even a moment's thought
They ask,
What Pataliputra?

Sir! You have to
answer them,
make them understand –
this is the same Pataliputra
for which
Ajatashatru, Bimbisara,
Chandragupta,
you and I
are fighting
Did you tell them?

Sir,
did you hear their retort?
'Fools
fighting for a fiction'

(1984)

SOME OTHER AMARAVATI

Maharaj
this is not that Amaravati
this is some
other Amaravati

No one's ready to fight for it
No one shouts
'I'll give my life
for Amaravati'

No one says
bursting with pride
'Amaravati is mine'

Maharaj
this is not the Amaravati
that till yesterday was yours

Now it is everyone's

The memories
have been erased,
the courtesans,
the stage,
the actors, the actresses
are nowhere to be seen

Maharaj!
Forget that Amaravati was ever yours,
even if it was
no one's ready to fight for it

(1984)

NALANDA

I'm going to Takshashila,
where
are you going?

Nalanda.

No,
this road
doesn't go to Nalanda,
it used to
once,
but not
any more.

The road to
Nalanda
has changed
now this
road will
take you
to Takshashila
not Nalanda.
Do you want to go to Takshashila?

Friends going to Nalanda,
often
it so happens that

the roads
you're shown
don't take you
where
you want to go —
like
Nalanda.

(1984)

WHY NOT MITHILA?

My king, don't be anxious —
anxiety makes the body
feeble,
the soul dull,
the voice weak.
Don't be anxious —

these are not reasons enough:
that in all of Mithila
there's not one poet,
that in the whole republic
there is no sculptor,
that Mithila would be complete
if it had but one singer

My king!
The presence or absence
of singers
makes no difference —

these are the things that matter:
wealth, armies, ministers,
the happiness
of your people.

Yes, Avanti has its
singers, sculptors, poets
but what are they doing?

My king! They say
they're creating Avanti –
that's how
they save themselves

They say the process never ends
Avanti is, Avanti will always be!

My king! I don't
understand –
Why has Mithila never been?
Why can Mithila never be?

(1984)

MATHURA'S LAMENT

Do you hear Mathura's lament?

This is what happens –

when Mathura is no more
Mathura cries
Mathura! Mathura!

Mathura is only one example –
take Avanti.
Listen carefully –

do you hear?
Every now and then
Avanti! Avanti!

It's like I said –
when Mathura is no more
when Avanti is no more
people cry Mathura! Avanti!

Maybe it has become
their habit to cry
when cities turn into memories

But –
Mathura and Avanti
are not memories

and even if they are,
will anyone believe
that Mathura and Avanti
are just memories?

(1984)

VAISHALI 1

There is only one name on the lips
of Vaishali's people –
Amrapali

Amrapali is happy that everyone
knows her
Amrapali is sad that
no one knows her

Those who do know
come to Vaishali
repeating Amrapali, Amrapali
the rest
keep away from Vaishali

People of Vaishali! Amrapali
is just an excuse –
those who know others
will come to Vaishali
chanting Amrapali, Amrapali

Those who don't want to know others –
will slip past Vaishali
saying the reason
is Amrapali

(1984

VAISHALI 2

We'll last, Vaishali will last
and if we don't?
Vaishali will last.

Vaishali is not a city
it is the memory
of those who came
before us –

of those who said
We'll last, Vaishali will last.
And if we don't?
Vaishali will last.

(1984)

THE REPUBLIC OF KOSAL

Kosal is a republic in my imagination
The people of Kosal are not happy
because Kosal is a republic only in the imagination.

The citizens
gamble all day
those who don't gamble
sleep

The citizens tell stories all day
those who don't tell stories
sleep

The citizens
are peevish all day
those who are not peevish
sleep

The citizens
rejoice
in Kosal's past
those who don't rejoice
sleep

Kosal is a republic in my imagination

(198

LACK OF THOUGHT
IN KOSAL

Maharaj, congratulations!
Maharaj, victory is yours!
There was no war –
the enemy turned back.

Our preparations, though, were thorough.
A four-akshauhini army,
ten thousand horses,
as many elephants.

No half measures!

Even if there had been a war
the outcome would've been the same.

They had no weapons,
no horses,
no elephants,
how could they have fought?
They were unarmed.

Each one of them was alone
and each one was saying
Everyone is alone.

All the same,
this is your victory!
Congratulations!
The rajasuya is complete
you have become emperor –

only, they've left behind some misgivings
for instance –

Kosal can't last much longer,
there's a lack of thought in Kosal

(198

THE STYLE OF KOSAL

Come outside Maharaj, outside
your glory
spreads like
        moonlight
Everyone is happy
No one says
        I have something to say

Something has happened
No one
      says anything
they're all afraid
      If ever they speak
they only say –
I am happy

Maharaj, haven't you wondered
how anyone
      can be happy and
not say a thing?

Anyway, Maharaj's glory
      spreads like moonlight
so where's the need
      to say anything?

But this much I will say
        Those who think
        speak out
and their speaking out
        becomes the style

The sad thing is
        that Kosal still
            still doesn't
                have a style of its ow

All the same,
        come outside
The crowd
        is saying in one voice –
We
    are happy!

Maharaj,
        as many times
as they tell you
tell them –
'My people!
        Stay happy'

(198

SHRAVASTI

Those who've left Shravasti
come back –

Mendicants still pass by
repeating
Those who've left
fearing sorrow
will find sorrow

Those who come
find sorrow
Those who go
find sorrow

There's as much sorrow in the rest of Kosal
as there is
in Shravasti

Those who've left Shravasti
come back –
Shravasti wants to say this
but can't

(1979)

THE LICCHAVIS

The Licchavis have gone the Licchavis will come bac

There'll be lights in the palaces
bangles will sound
from the inner chambers

there'll be markets
there'll be auctions
there'll be alms
there'll be beggars
there'll be desires
there'll be desirers

Then why are the widows sad?
Why is Vaishali silent?

The truth is that the Licchavis will never come

Even if they do
                they'll only say
We were the Licchavis, we are the Licchavis
and so saying
                they'll pass

The Licchavis are not common
that's why they are the Licchavis

(197

VASANTASENA

Vasantasena
is climbing the stairs

You won't understand now
Vasantasena,
you are still young

The stairs never
end
whether of progress
or
regress

of arrival
or
departure
or
fall
or
pride

You won't
understand now
Vasantasena

Neither is
ascent
easy

nor
descent,
the stairs
we ascend
are the stairs
we have
to descend

The stairs are indifferent,

who goes up
who goes down
who goes
up then down
or down then up
how many
have been ascended
how many are left
to descend

they neither count
nor hear

Vasantasena!

(19

AMBAPALI

Vaishali sleeps soundly,
only
Ambapali
is awake

It's dark
in some other world
morning
comes
slowly

Stars fall

In Vaishali
people are born
people die

Vaishali sleeps
or
has she died
Ambapali
is frightened
in her dream

Don't be frightened, Ambapali!

(1979)

HORSEMAN

Is a horseman
who goes to Kalinga
the same when he returns?

What do people call him –
victor
        or murderer?
Is he
welcomed by
                courtesans
or
does he drift aimlessly?

What happens?

Horseman,
where does this road go?

(197

TRAUMA

A full moon night.
A full moon.
A mirror.

In the mirror
looking just like
the moon
the moon's
reflection.

After resting
for a while
the moon
slowly
moved
out
of
the doorway.

I said,
How
silent it is!
Just then
I saw her
in
the mirror —

before I
could
ask,
Who are you,
she
had
already
disappeared.

Years later
remembering
that day
that
incident
it strikes me —
she was
Padmini!

'That's why,'
I say,
'That's why
we are
both
broken,
the mirror
and
I.'

(198

COMING AND GOING

Whenever he went
from Kosal to Magadh
from Magadh to Kosal
everyone asked him
the same question –

Are you going
from Magadh to Kosal
or are you coming
from Kosal to Magadh?

What's the difference,
he would say
and try
to evade the question.

But some
questions
can't be evaded –
especially when
we often pass
through Kosal on the way to Magadh
or through Magadh on the way to Kosal.

It's the most important question of all –
Where are you going?

Who
are you looking for
in Kosal and in Magadh?

And
will Kosal
come first
or Magadh?

The truth is
no one knows why
he keeps coming and going
from Magadh to Kosal
from Kosal to Magadh.

Why does he play out the same scenes
over and over again?

Why
does he shout slogans
for Kosal
when passing through Magadh,
against Magadh
when passing through Kosal?

Why
does he raise

over the crumbling forts of Kosal
the tattered flags
of Magadh?

When no answers
are forthcoming
he too
joins those
who grab passers-by
and ask –

Are you passing
through Kosal
on the way to Magadh
or
through Magadh
on the way to Kosal?

(1984)

QUESTIONS FROM FRIENDS

Friends,
it is meaningless
to say I'm coming back.

The question is: where are you headed?

Friends,
it is pointless
to say I'm moving with the times.

The question is: are the times changing you
or are you
changing the times?

Friends,
it is meaningless
to say I've reached home.

The question is:
where will you go now?

(1984)

SHADOW

Years later I found out
that the one
still with me
was not a shadow

I trampled it
it cried
I called it
it was coy
I scolded it
it wrapped itself
around my legs
I said
Stop following me
it faltered

I took my place
in the council
it sat
by my
side

The council
is gone
the assemblies
have fled
The one still with me
can't be a shadow

(1979)

OFFERING

I could have saved myself
but how could I
Those who save themselves
cannot create

I simmered
then blazed
I began to crack

I could have cried out
but how could I
Those who cry
cannot sustain

It was not self-sacrifice
not resignation
not self-abuse
not castigation
What
was it then

I could have blamed someone
but how could I
Those who blame cannot create

(1979

DISILLUSIONMENT OF A COURTESAN FROM THE TIME OF THE BUDDHA

With each caress
the breasts quiver

From the navel a fragrance rises

Astride
these thighs
only the mighty
can ride their
horse into the river

In search of unending pleasure come
the general,
the prince.

Women swoon.

Malati,
it won't be the same tomorrow
The breasts
will be filled
with pus,
the thighs
will lie broken
like monuments

You'll only be able
to hear footsteps –
whose?
The general's?
Or the prince's?

The river of pleasure
will have run dry

They'll joke
those who rode their
horse –
you too will laugh.

Fetching a corpse from the river
people leave it
at the ghats
and say –
Here lies Time

No one sees Malati.

With each caress
the breasts
quivered.

Only the mighty
straddled
these thighs.
In search of
unending pleasure
came the prince.

Women
swooned.

The irony
Malati,
you'll always be
Malati.

(1984)

BY THE GRACE OF MAHAKAAL

Half cry, half laugh
they all live in Avanti

by the grace of Mahakaal

Half believe that being incomplete
is as meaningful
as being complete

Half claim that being complete
is as meaningless
as being incomplete

Half are speechless, half debate
they all live in Avanti

by the grace of Mahakaal

Half say that Avanti
is incomplete in
the same way as Kashi,

half say that only
immigrants live
in both cities

They all get trapped in their own argument
they all live in Avanti

They laugh
Kashi's pundits at Avanti's learning
Avanti's people at Kashi's assumptions

by the grace of Mahakaal

(1984)

ROOT

Why are you silent, friends?

What's happened in Magadh?

Has the king died?
Or has the queen given birth to a girl again?

Has war been declared once more?
Have sanctions been imposed once more?

What's happened?
Why are you silent?

Was the antidote useless?
Is there no one left in Magadh?

No one knows
what happens to Magadh sometimes
All will be well yet
no one will say anything
no one will open their mouths
Only Shaktar
who can tell a tree
by its roots
thinks and is terrified

Friends,
whoever thinks
will be terrified

(1984)

WAILING FROM THE INNER CHAMBERS

Why is there wailing from the inner chambers?

Ask,
find out
Maharaj
wants to know –

When
sparks
of happiness
fly all around,

when everyone
thinks
of their own
advancement,

why this sorrow?

When
everyone
says
what happened
was right,

why this repentance?

When
everyone
behaves
themselves,

when
everyone
thinks before
they speak,

why these tirades?

Find out.

(1984)

HE WHO WAS YOUNG

Everyone will return
except he
who was young —
youth does not return.

Even if he does
he won't be the same.

White hair, wrinkles,
senility,
fatigue
He will have become old.

It's natural
for a man to grow old
along the way —
whether the way be easy or hard

Why would anyone want
to be called old?

Why would anyone
count his
white hairs?

Why would anyone
want to be surprised
by the wrinkles on his face?

Why would anyone want
to be told
How quickly a man can grow old –
for example, you!

Why would anyone want
to become
an exemplar of senility, death and fatigue?

Everyone will return
except he
who was young.

(1984)

THE DOM OF MANIKARNIKA

The dom often tells Manikarnika,
Manikarnika
don't be sad,
sadness does not become you
There are burning ghats
where not one corpse arrives
and even if it does,
it isn't bathed
                    in the Ganga

What else
can the dom say,
who else
but a dom can stay
alone
at Manikarnika

Manikarnika, don't be sad,
sadness is not
for you
It is for those
who come here
it was for those
they leave behind

Yet they are fortunate
they get to leave
their sadness to you
Manikarnika

Manikarnika
don't be sad,

sadness does not become us

There are doms
whose eyes turn to stone
waiting for corpses
but no corpse arrives –

what else can the dom say?

(1984)

A JUST WAR

How is it possible
for the number of dead to be the same on both side

How is it possible
for the flag to fall
on both sides
For the widows
on one side
to outnumber
the unwidowed
on the other

How is it possible
for the sorrow in one capital
to equal
the mourning
in the other

That there be repentance
on both sides
That there be dharma
on both sides
That there be shame
on both sides
That both sides
lay down their arms
That both be victorious

I say
it is not possible

One-sided the murders
the victory one-sided

One-sided the arrogance
the fear one-sided

One-sided the widows
the unwidowed one-sided

One-sided the sorrow
the mourning one-sided

One-sided the joy
the repentance one-sided

One-sided the dharma
the shame one-sided

The number of dead on both sides
is never the same

(1984)

DESTINATION: CHAMPA

We have to go only to Champa

This road goes only to Champa
Those who have to go elsewhere
should go by other roads
they should not confuse us by asking –
Does this road go to Champa?

Those who have to go to Champa
have no right to ask anything –
Not: where is Champa?
Not: where isn't Champa?
Not: what is Champa?
Not: is it true
that Champa was
and is no more?

We have to go only to Champa

(19̶

PEOPLE GOING TO KANNAUJ

Brothers and sisters, where are you going?
We are all
going to Kannauj,
because everyone
is going to Kannauj

Those going nowhere,
are going to Kannauj
Those going here and there,
are going to Kannauj

Those who love Kannauj
are going to Kannauj,
those who hate Kannauj
are going to Kannauj

Those who know nothing
about Kannauj
are going to Kannauj
Those who know everything
about Kannauj
are going to Kannauj

Who isn't going to Kannauj?

(1984)

THE LAW

I say again, Maharaj —
do not say,
'The law can't be changed.
What applies to others
applies to me as well.'

There are other ways
to confound the council —
the truth is unnecessary
it is unwise
to be prodigal with the truth —

if you must, say
'The law can't be broken,
the law
can be changed.'

Say
'I don't break the law
like everyone
I fear it
But sometimes, citizens,
when it starts to smother
I make
amendments —
the law, after all, can be relaxed.'

(19

PATALIPUTRA

A smear of blood upon the forehead
that is the way
                    coronations are done

Whose blood is it?
Not his,
the star of
            Magadh's eye?

Whose
        blood is it?
Does
     it
        matter?
Even a star
            can sometimes
pierce
        the
            eye

The Mauryas don't care
                        for ill omens
the Mauryas
              care
                  for victory

Between Takshashila and Nalanda
there are
        the Mauryas
                and there is
                        the road

The
    flag
        flutters

It's not
        just
            the Mauryas
                who are
                    to blame

even earlier
        the pundits
            had said –

The
    night
        deepens
            in
                Pataliputra

(19

A YEAR OF POEMS

What I wrote, useless
What I did not,
                    meaningless

(1984)

INTERFERENCE

No one even sneezes
for fear
of disrupting
peace in Magadh,
peace must remain in Magadh
if Magadh
is to remain

If there's Magadh, there's peace

No one even screams
for fear
of disrupting
order in Magadh
Order must remain in Magadh

Where will it be
if not in Magadh?

What will people say?

But what of people?
They even say
that Magadh is now Magadh
only in name

No one even interrupts
for fear
of interruption
becoming the custom in Magadh

Once it starts
interference never stops –

and whatever you do
people of Magadh
you can't escape interference –

if nothing else
a dead body
passing through the city
will interfere, asking –
Why do people die?

(1984)

RELEASE

I want to go to Kashi,
I say
I'm going to Kosal

What's there in Kashi –
there's Manikarnika
corpses come
corpses go

I don't want to go to Kashi

I want to go to Kashi

I say
Unfortunate is he
who goes to Kashi
not Kosal

You've seen Kosal
so come
I'm going to Kosal

There's a difference
between Kosal
and Kashi –
Kosal is not Kashi

I want to die
in Kosal
I say –

Fortunate are they who
find release
in Kashi

(1984)

SHAKTAR

Shaktar! Shaktar!
Shaktar isn't here.
Maybe he's gone towards Takshashila.

Shaktar! Shaktar!
Shaktar isn't here.
Maybe he's returned to Magadh.

Shaktar! Shaktar!
Shaktar isn't in Magadh, or in Takshashila.
You won't find Shaktar anywhere.

Shaktar comes only
when Chandragupta comes.

Shaktar kills
Chandragupta embraces,
sometimes Chandragupta kills
Shaktar lowers his head

Shaktar isn't in Magadh, or in Takshashila.

(1९

THE THIRD WAY

Voices in Magadh say no rulers remain in Magadh
Those that were there
thanks to liquor, stupidity and laziness
are no longer
                worthy
of being called
                Magadh's rulers

Voices
            in Avanti
in Kosal
            in Vidarbha
            say the same
There are
            no rulers

Those that were there
thanks to liquor, stupidity and laziness
are
    no longer
    worthy
of being called our rulers
What do we do then?

If there are no rulers
                there'll be no law

If there's no law
　　　　there'll be no order

If there's no order
　　　　there'll be no dharma

If there's no dharma
　　　　there'll be no society

If there's no society
　　　　there'll be no individual

If there are no individuals
　　　　we won't exist

What do we do?

Break the law?

　　　　Forget dharma?

　　　　　　Disrupt the order?

Friends,
there are only
　　　　two ways:
　　　　　　we can act unethically
　　　　　　　　and keep
　　　　　　　　　debating ethi◂

Act immorally
            and keep
                        debating morality

Speak untruth
            practise untruth
                        live untruth –

and keep pretending
            to wage wars for truth

                        In the end
                        everyone
                                    has to die

but we shouldn't
            give our lives
                        without reason

Friends,
there's also
            a third way –

but
    it doesn't go
    through
            Magadh,
                        Avanti
                                    Kosal
                        or
                        Vidarbha.

(1984)

THE ILLUSION

In my youth
if I chanced upon
some old man
leaning on a stick
crossing the road
clutching his heart

I'd pray
for myself,
Lord!
Take me
before I get old

Now I am old
leaning on a stick
crossing the road
clutching my heart

I pray –

Not yet!
Let me at least cross
the road

Listen my fellow traveller,
here,
take

my hand –
help me
across the road

(1984)

PROOF

Leaving their footprints in the sand
they ask, the next day –
Where has the proof
of our travels gone?

Do you know
what answer
they get?

Brothers, go
where
there's no sand

no one can leave
their mark
on sand

(19

RETURN

I saw him leave
by this very road:

he was not alone,
there was an army,
elephants,
horses,
chariots,
music –
the works.

And him
in the midst of it all
on horseback
serene
passing by,
as if
he
was in charge,
and the rest
merely
following.

Twenty years later
I see him
return
by this very road:

he is not alone,
there is an army,
elephants,
horses,
chariots,
music —
the works.

And him
in the midst of it all
on horseback
serene
passing by,
as if
someone else
is in charge,
and
he
merely following.

(19

ENCOUNTER

Whose reflection do we see in the river
that startles us,
that makes us scream:
No, this can't be true!

But it is true

and we
can only reassure ourselves:
It was an illusion:
this is no river,
this is not the one
the mere sight of whom
can shock us.

We can't
escape the river

It will come to us
in dreams,
it will remind us
You'll be
startled,
you'll scream:
This is the one
escaping from whom
I used to say,
I'm grateful!

(1984)

ROHITASHVA

Whenever you go to Manikarnika
you'll find an old man
huddled in a corner.

Seeing you
something
in his eyes
will light up –

crying
Rohitashva, Rohitashva,
he
will embrace you

Then what will you say?

This, right:
'I'm not Rohitashva
I really
am not
Rohitashva.'

But how
will you convince
the old man
that you
are not Rohitashva?

His hold on you
will get stronger,
he'll exclaim,
'You really are Rohitashva!'

How will you
convince him
whose Rohitashva
is dead
that you
are not Rohitashva?

(1984)

NAME ON THE WALL

When I was a child
I'd write
my name
in chalk
on every blank wall
I came across

The next day I'd find
someone had rubbed it out
so thoroughly
as if it had never been written

Then I'd shout –
Who did this?
I'd get the answer –
Somadatta

I
am old now
I write
my name
in chalk
on every blank wall
I come across

The next day I find
someone has rubbed it out

so thoroughly
as if it had never been written

Now when I shout –
Who did this?
I get the answer –
Time

(1984)

SHRIKANT VERMA'S *MAGADH* AND THE NAYI KAVITA MOVEMENT

is English translation of Shrikant Verma's 1984 poetry volume, *igadh*, by Rahul Soni should bring back some necessary atten-n to a period in Hindi writing known for both its formal experi-ntation and its political vigour. The Nayi Kavita (new poetry) vement in Hindi, beginning well before Indian Independence, ered in an ethic of writing that was highly innovative yet ted in the everyday, much like *Magadh*. The movement con-ses with varied historical and literary realities, providing us h a rich context in which to understand Verma's work.

Magadh remains one of the most minimal and sparsely written umes of Hindi poetry, a serial poem in many ways. Verma, n in Bilaspur in 1931, not only became one of the most prom-nt figures of Nayi Kavita but also played a key role in Indira ndhi's government during the Emergency – he is said to have ned the infamous slogan 'Garibi Hatao' (Reduce Poverty) t in practice became 'Garib Hatao' (Reduce the Poor). Soni, riter–translator, has, among other achievements, also edited anthology of Hindi poetry and translated Geetanjali Shree's el *The Roof Beneath Their Feet*. With *Magadh*, a book now ly available or written about even in Hindi, Soni's job as a slator becomes far more urgent. His translations of Verma's der, cyclical verse should serve as a discovery for readers ndian and modernist poetry everywhere.

Soni's achievement as a translator lies in his ability to esca
a certain literalness and verbosity of previous and partial trai
lations of *Magadh*, a practice emerging perhaps from the ne
to spell out the historical context for Anglophone reade
but also from the formal urge to smoothen some of the criti
clumsiness of the original Hindi verse. Soni's English trans
tion, while being attuned to the formal sparseness of *Maga*
is also sharply aware of its verbal intonation and oddity. Sor
translation echoes this original voice, but it also speaks in
own lilt and creates a strange new idiom in English.

The circular quality of some of the poems, their shre
wordplay and an array of historical references makes the coll
tion, otherwise written in everyday Hindi, seem a little dista
Although Verma's language, his diction and syntax, offers
resistance to comprehension whatsoever, it is quite difficult to
down these poems thematically. The temporal gap between or
literal reading of the poem and an insight into its metaphori
and symbolic significance, if any, is the real challenge of read
Magadh. The poem 'Coming and Going' is a case in point:

> Whenever he went
> from Kosal to Magadh
> from Magadh to Kosal
> everyone asked him
> the same question –
>
> Are you going
> from Magadh to Kosal
> or are you coming
> from Kosal to Magadh?

What's the difference,
he would say
and try
to evade the question.

But some
questions
can't be evaded –
especially when
we often pass
through Kosal on the way to Magadh
or through Magadh on the way to Kosal.

It's the most important question of all –
Where are you going?

Who
are you looking for
in Kosal and in Magadh?

And
will Kosal
come first
or Magadh?

ile the above lines might strike one as a parodic attempt to
her the confusion between 'coming' and 'going', which is what
 in a way, it is also a formally playful way to question the
ility of certain spaces in history. The two ancient kingdoms
Magadh and Kosal, both of which find an important place in

Hindu mythology, are different in their claims to power. Wh
Kosal was the centre of power during the Treta Yuga (the seco
of the four ages articulated in Hinduism) as described in t
Ramayana, Magadh during the Dwapara Yuga (the third a
under Jarasandha (the king of Magadh and an ardent devo
of Shiva) became the authoritarian force in the Indo-Gange
plains and caused the exodus of various Bhoja tribes to Kos
Later, the Pandavas travelled from Kosal to Magadh (not t
other way round) in order to conquer Jarasandha's kingdo
Thus, the question here of 'coming' and 'going' hints at t
larger osmosis of power played throughout history, where
source of one's journey is as much a deciding factor in on
fate as one's destination. In Verma's case, as we'd later see, t
walking between ancient Indian kingdoms is painstakin
perpetual.

*

While conducting a series of video interviews with the cr
Rajendra Mishra about the development of Hindi literat
in Chhattisgarh, I heard him talk about his encounter w
Shrikant Verma in the 1950s, while the latter was still teach
at a high school in Bilaspur. One of the things he remembe
was Verma sitting in front of a local laundry centre, reading
poems from journals published around the time. This laun
centre in a provincial town of central India, perhaps wit
small sitting area in one corner, became the place where Ver
acquainted himself with the exciting new changes in Hi
poetry – which he was soon to join after publishing his f
collection of verse, *Bhatka Megh* (1957).

By the time he shifted to Delhi, which was in the early 1960s,
was already being recognised as one of the central figures of
ayi Kavita. And if Mishra is to be believed, this geographical
d intellectual drift from a small town to the very centre of
wer is what governs the logic of *Magadh*. According to him,
en after being comfortably settled in Delhi for more than
o decades, Verma was in a state of crisis while complet-
g this collection. An elected member of the Rajya Sabha, a
sonal adviser to the Indian prime minister Indira Gandhi
ring the Emergency and the spokesperson for the Congress
rty during this time, Verma was visibly successful in poli-
s, and thus it came as a slight surprise to me when Mishra
st revealed a certain anxiety, a geographical and cultural
enation, that he saw in Verma and his body of work. The
em 'Nameless in Avanti' can be read in this context, where
anti possibly symbolises Bilaspur, as Magadh stands in
Delhi:

> Will it make a difference
> if I say
> I'm not from Magadh
> I'm from Avanti?
>
> Of course it will
> you'll be taken to belong to Avanti
> you'll have to forget Magadh
>
> And you
> will not be able to forget Magadh
> you'll live your life

in Avanti
without knowing Avanti

Then you'll say
I'm not from Avanti
I'm from Magadh
and no one will believe you
You'll cry –
'It's true
I'm from Magadh
I'm not from Avanti'
and it will make no difference

No one will believe you are
from Magadh
No one will recognise you
in Avanti

Hindi poetry addressed the issues of postcolonial modernity
a fashion different from Indian English writing or other region
literatures, in that it did not have to negotiate the burdens
an inherited colonial language, culture or readership, nor w
its scope confined to a particular linguistic state or region
Poetry in modern Hindi was starting to be written between t
final decade of the nineteenth century and the first decade
the twentieth century. The compositions before that, writt
in medieval Hindi dialects, were either devotional in natu
or addressed the themes of erotic and courtly love, the lat
also inflecting the courtesan poems in *Magadh*. These compo
tions, still used in Hindustani classical music, started to app

ring the Bhakti and Riti periods and were used as standard
otifs by individual poets and connoisseurs until the end of the
neteenth century. This shift towards vernacular forms, in the
akti and Riti periods, was instrumental in shaping Hindi as a
erary language. Among the many texts that contributed to this
olution, Tulsidas's *Ramcharitmanas* – his sixteenth-century
vadhi retelling of the *Ramayana* – played a pivotal role in
ving the way for the consolidation of modern Hindi.

This process of formalisation was arguably strengthened with
at is known as the Dwivedi Yuga (the age of Dwivedi), named
er the immensely influential writer Mahavir Prasad Dwivedi.
voting most of his literary life to the cause of modern Hindi,
edited the magazine *Saraswati* from 1903, which for the next
enteen years promoted and published poets with 'modern
nsibilities'. These poets, more often than not, subscribed to
lorious vision of India's past and assiduously wrote about
geographical uniqueness and natural splendour. The foci
devotional poetry, Krishna and Radha, were now replaced
a celebratory, yet arbitrary, idea of India and its history.
ithilisharan Gupt's *Bharat-Bharati* (Voice of India) and
ridhar Pathak's *Bharatgeet* (Songs of India) are comprehensive
mples of this age. Preceded by writers such as Bhartendu
rishchandra, Dwivedi's contribution lies in his determined
ort to establish modern Hindi as a literary language, wedded,
nis conception, to patriotism and the nation state.

The contrast between Verma's ideas on ancient India and that
he poets of the Dwivedi Yuga can be easily noted when one
ks at how *Magadh* maps a slim and banal landscape of these
ner kingdoms, and constantly undercuts the stability and
mony that are foundational for a grand narrative. It is also

the difference between writers writing before and after Indi
Independence in 1947. The former, working with only an inkli
of independent India and with questions of nationhood loomi
large, fantasised about an allegorical nation almost as an impei
tive, while the post-Independence writers, with an eye on comm
nal violence and a certain disillusionment with Nehruvian soci
ism, challenged the erstwhile optimism towards the nation st
in multiple ways. This is how the poem 'Corpses in Kashi', set i
city that prides itself on its ritualistic and sacred qualities, begi

> Have you seen Kashi?
> Where
> corpses come and
> corpses go
> by the same road.
>
> And what of corpses?
> Corpses will come,
> corpses will go –
>
> ask then, Whose corpse is this?
> Rohitashva's?
> No, no,
> all corpses can't be Rohitashva

However, not all pre-Independence literatures were natior
istic, or nationalistic in the same mould. Chhayavaad, the
of Romanticism in Hindi poetry, prompted verses with d
humanist and mystical elements while embracing a perso
vision. This meant doing away with formal constraints, l

yming couplets and strict metrical patterns, imposed by earlier
ovements. The impact of these poets, or rather their context,
n be imagined by the notoriety they gained merely for writing
e verse. It is this formal experimentation and freedom that
ayi Kavita owes to Chhayavaad writers. A modern Marxist
et and major practitioner of Nayi Kavita, Gajanan Madhav
uktibodh, published a long study of Jaishankar Prasad's *Kamayani*,
e of the masterpieces of Chhayavaad writing, claiming it to
one of his stylistic influences. Nevertheless, on the surface,
hayavaad consciously maintained an apolitical stance, often
uating its subjects in trans-historical and mythological idylls.
This lack of political commitment came under sharp critique
m Pragativaad (the Progressive movement), which emerged
the 1930s with the formation of the Progressive Writers'
sociation in 1936. Inspired by socialist ideas of revolution
d aesthetics, these writers made sure that they wrote in a
nmon idiom and represented a large group of people. Some
the major works of this period, especially poetry, shifted the
ce from an individual 'hero' back to society, and embodied a
ict ethics of revolution and change. However, the movement
d its own problems as it soon became artistically didactic
d ideologically constrained. These issues, too complex to
er here fully, are what provoked Nayi Kavita to experiment
mally, while at the same time being politically rooted. The
ets of Nayi Kavita were not only politically conscious but,
the Pragativaad poets, also active participants in political
nge. Thus, when Shrikant Verma, who was at the forefront of
ctoral politics for almost a decade, wrote 'Lack of Thought in
sal', it almost read as a satire of the very political formations
which he was a beneficiary:

Maharaj, congratulations!
Maharaj, victory is yours!
There was no war –
the enemy turned back.

Our preparations, though, were thorough.
A four-akshauhini army,
ten thousand horses,
as many elephants.

No half measures!

Even if there had been a war
the outcome would've been the same.

They had no weapons,
no horses,
no elephants,
how could they have fought?
They were unarmed.

Each one of them was alone
and each one was saying
Everyone is alone.

All the same,
this is your victory!
Congratulations!
The rajasuya is complete
you have become emperor –

only, they've left behind some misgivings
for instance –

Kosal can't last much longer,
there's a lack of thought in Kosal

ᴉe more radical of the modern poets, Muktibodh and Dhoomil,
:spite their affiliations with progressive values, decided to
:nture outside the didactic format of Pragativaad. Lucy
ɔsenstein, who translated some of the key writers of Nayi
ıvita in her anthology *New Poetry in Hindi* (2003), notes how
ᴇ aesthetics of the movement allowed for, or rather creatively
ıpported, heterogeneous themes and ideas. Unlike other
ᴇrary movements, Nayi Kavita did not invest its energies
ᴛo creating a stylistic or political unity. In 1943, Agyeya,
ıe of the major figures of modern Indian poetry, published
ɜlim anthology known as *Tar Saptak* which contained one
the first traces of Nayi Kavita. In his introduction, Agyeya
ᴉites:

They have not reached any destination, they are still trav-
ellers – not even travellers, but seekers of a path. There
is no ideological unity among them, their opinions on all
important subjects . . . are different.

ᴉnong the poets included in *Tar Saptak* were Marxists like
ᴜktibodh and Freudians like Agyeya himself. It was unique
ᴇn for Hindi literature to have a movement based purely on
ᴉistic affiliations without a unity of ideas or ideology. Shrikant
rma, who does not find a place in Rosenstein's anthology,

was one of the several independent voices who came together under the banner of Nayi Kavita.

Nayi Kavita also made possible a shift in Hindi poetry towards a more material understanding of the self as shaped by social and psychological forces. In Agyeya's own words 'During the interwar period a . . . profound change had been developing. It was not purely subjective like Chhayavaad, nor merely objective-correlative like Pragativaad, but a basic reorientation towards man. It was a growing awareness . . . of the integrity of the human individual.' While this individualist strain echoes some of the concerns of European modernism, the 'reorientation' attempted in Nayi Kavita was also directly linked to several local crises, including the changing industrial, urban conditions of a postcolonial India, the scarring violence of Partition, the failure of Nehruvian ideas and, more specifically, the history of political commitment in Hindi poetry and its relationship with individualism. 'Questions from Friends', one of the few 'personal' poems in *Magadh*, tersely articulates an anxiety perhaps shared by millions right after Independence:

> Friends,
> it is meaningless
> to say I'm coming back.
>
> The question is: where are you headed?
>
> Friends,
> it is pointless
> to say I'm moving with the times.

The question is: are the times changing you
or are you
changing the times?

Friends,
it is meaningless
to say I've reached home.

The question is:
where will you go now?

ɔsenstein lists 'the wonderment of everyday life, the iron-
s of daily existence, communion with nature, musings over
ɹilosophical issues, the experience of the creative process,
ienation and social inequality' as the major thematic con-
rns of Nayi Kavita. All the above categories hold equally
ɹe for *Magadh*, but not before one wades through the pri-
ɑry complexities of its 'allegorical' narrative. The themes
ɑt Rosenstein mentions wouldn't seem necessary at all if
ɹe were to read the poems merely for their narrative quality.
ɹe difficulty of pinning down these poems thematically, as
ɛntioned earlier, is their inviting narrative scheme and their
ɛtaphorical subtlety. Thus, poems like 'Destination: Champa'
ɹd 'Ujjaini', on the first reading, might just suggest a physical
ɹplacement of the places mentioned in their titles. A closer
ɔk might also indicate the state of a dispossessed traveller
ɹ whom the sociocultural meaning of a physical destination,
ɹich has probably also become a figment of the imagina-
ɹn, has been either lost or institutionally barred. One can
ɹd 'Destination: Champa', its stern denial of any curiosity

regarding the actual nature of the destination, as marking th
transition:

> Those who have to go to Champa
> have no right to ask anything –
> Not: where is Champa?
> Not: where isn't Champa?
> Not: what is Champa?
> Not: is it true
> that Champa was
> and is no more?

*

Sridala Swami, reviewing the translation for the *Sunday Guardia*
talks of how Verma's involvement in and experience of nation
politics are 'expressed in often disquieting ways' in some of t
poems. To elucidate this point, Swami quotes from the poe
'Interference', where lines like 'peace must remain in Magad
'Order must remain in Magadh' and 'What will people sa
create a sense of forced harmony and order that is impos
on Magadh, where any kind of interference is to be avoid
at all costs. The poem ends by naming death as the ultima
interference, for which Magadh's systematic governance w
have no answers. This is where the catastrophic quality
Magadh is laid bare, to be feared and accepted. Verma, w
can claim to have an insider's view of power politics, se
annihilation, in this poem and several others, as the only w
out of an illusory order. None of the poems effectively resto
our faith in any kind social mobilisation or change, and

ear of Poems', quoted here in its entirety of three lines, is a
ood example:

> What I wrote, useless
> What I did not,
> > meaningless

this case, how does one read *Magadh*, whose understanding
politics is deeply pessimistic, as a statement on the political
e of Shrikant Verma? In a piece published in the *Oxonian*
view, Nakul Krishna hints at a kind of expiation that Verma
ight be looking for through the collection. By 1984, the year
nen *Magadh* was first published, the true nature and extent
the violence practised during the Emergency years were
dely known facts. Verma's complicity as the mouthpiece for
e government during these years and possibly an eventual
lf-realisation are what made *Magadh* appear at the time it did
d say the things it said.

However, it would be a mistake to read *Magadh* merely for its
tobiographical or confessional elements. A more important
ea to look at would be the treatment of the common citizens
no populate these poems. By representing them as dormant
ures placed at the receiving end of institutional power, Verma
nies them any substantial agency except by virtue of their
n passivity. The arbitrary institutions that run these ancient
ngdoms of Kashi, Magadh, Kosal and Vaishali, among others,
em to have certain absolute arrangements already in place.
hile the corpses in Kashi 'come and go by the same road',
sal's people, in the absence of a republic, are shown to be
dlessly rejoicing in their past. Similarly, the greatest fear in

'Some Other Amaravati' is that the people do not believe
fighting for their kingdom any more. Although Krishna right
reads the message in these poems as carrying 'a strong whiff
bad faith', they also extend the scope and theme of the colle
tion, which in its 'Invocation' promises to narrate the sorrov
of both cities and citizens.

If *Magadh*'s subject matter offers us a labyrinth of political an
historical allusions, its form cleanly departs from its conter
containing a witty, ironical energy. While some of the lines
Magadh are in the form of pithy sayings like 'Is a horseman
who goes to Kalinga / the same when he returns?', others appe
to be roadside conversations: 'Horseman, / where does this ro:
go?' Nayi Kavita, and its endorsement of free verse and rhyth
as multilayered concepts, has clearly been important in Verm:
oeuvre. But *Magadh* is an exception even among Verma's oth
works, none of which achieve the terse urgency and repetiti
clarity of the volume. While Chhayavaad as a movement sh
conventional rhyme and metre, championing free verse, a
Nayi Kavita innovated with various kinds of poetic modes a
asymmetric formal constructions, *Magadh* is a landmark work
this context for its exploration of contemporary speech, ecc
omised phrasing and novel use of repetition. The title poe
'Magadh', depends on these techniques to create a gritty ser
of desolation and forgetfulness:

> Listen horseman, where's Magadh?
> I've come
> from Magadh
> I must go to
> Magadh

Where
do I turn?
North or south,
east or west?

Here I see Magadh,
here it disappears –

just yesterday
I left Magadh
just yesterday
Magadh's people
told me not to
leave Magadh
I gave my word –
I'd be back
before sunrise

But there is
neither Magadh nor Magadh
You too have been searching,
brothers,
this is not the Magadh
you've read about
in books,
this is the Magadh
that you
like me
have lost

*

To walk a city is to see it at once from a distance, as a Euclidea
marker on a map, and as a lived instance of plurality, uneve
ness and contingencies. In this venture of walking, one is bo
a planner or navigator and vulnerable to plans that are alrea
in place. A poem like 'The Road to Ujjaini', which appears
a public announcement, has at its core the duality of walki
experience. More or less, Ujjaini is an idea or feeling which n
everyone achieves by taking the same road. The surreal poten
of Ujjaini is marked, surprisingly, by the non-teleological cha
acteristics of the road.

> All travellers going to Ujjaini:
> this road does not go to Ujjaini
> and this same road goes to Ujjaini
>
> Till yesterday I'd show the way
> saying
> Attention! This road goes to Ujjaini
> I show the way today as well
> saying
> Attention! This road does not go to Ujjaini
>
> Travellers!
> The truth is that
> every road goes to Ujjaini
> and that
> no road goes to Ujjaini

Ujjaini
forever looks to the road
Ujjaini
has turned away from roads

Then
where should those going to Ujjaini go?
They should go to Ujjaini
and say,
This is not Ujjaini
because we
did not arrive here on the roads
that go to Ujjaini
or on the roads
that don't go to Ujjaini

ichel de Certeau, in his famous work *The Practice of Everyday* *fe*, notes: 'Thus the street geometrically defined by urban anning is transformed into a space by walkers. In the same ly, an act of reading is the space produced by the practice of particular place: a written text, i.e., a place constituted by a stem of signs.' Even if *Magadh*, due to its allegorical design, es not seem to tackle questions of space directly from the int of view of an individual, it does make an effort to dis-guish a place from space. The crux of such an effort lies in polyvalent approach to places with fixed names and asso-tions. Thus, the person who walks the landscape of *Magadh* ceives these places not as they would be meant to be received lturally, but as floating signifiers of various other things, like e birth cycle, urban desperation and totalitarianism.

The ancient kingdoms that we see as titles for many of th
poems are not merely historical places to hang a narrative aroun
but fluid spaces which mutate in meaning and form. The poet
persona walks around and towards these spaces, asking f
directions ('Horseman'), observing rituals ('The Style of Kosal
and attributing totemic values ('Return'). These places, whic
have their mythic significance, are already removed from the po
physically and historically. To describe them in terms of wh
remains of them for us, like ruins, coins or texts, would only l
making them locations to be visited and objectively appreciate
unlike the 'walkable' spaces that *Magadh* creates for its narrate
By bending certain rules of logic and cartography, Verma maj
a more personalised space of everyday experience, while n
making any insistent efforts to index these experiences in actu
historical events. Lines like 'Before Kosambi / there was only
Kosambi,' and 'after Kosambi / there is only / Kosambi' crea
a haunting dialectic of transience and permanence. Kosaml
where the Buddha lived for two years, and which, legend has
was founded by Brahma's grandson Kushamba, is envisione
as a timeless place, unchanged by the passage of the centurie
However, this sense of permanence is also unsettled by tl
narrator's awareness of a 'before' and 'after', the germ of histo
suggesting that Kosambi's fixity is not absolute.

*

The seriality in *Magadh* is upheld by the formal and themat
similarity of the poems, but also by their common attention
places, mythical and ancient, that are on the verge of losing th
cultural and political significance. Their fall into decaden

nd an ultimate disappearance is what conjoins them in the
ollection. We see the impending doom in the behaviour of
ings (Amaravati) and the populace (Kosal) alike, but what we
o not witness in the poems is the actual point of decimation
f these glorious kingdoms. Even walking, an everyday practice,
ppears to be a circular and tedious exercise, where the people
re shorn of any capacity to choose their own destinations. In
he poem titled 'People Going to Kannauj' lines such as 'Those
oing nowhere, / are going to Kannauj / Those going here and
here, / are going to Kannauj' empty any intentionality on the
art of the travellers. The rest of the poem continues with the
heme of people walking to Kannauj without any real purpose
r effort. If the cities in *Magadh* are half dead, and this is how
hey are fated to remain, the process of walking is already
oomed. The everyday is caught in its own web of repetition
nd myopia as the larger world around it faces the challenge
f survival. This might be what Arvind Krishna Mehrotra had
n mind when he described *Magadh* as 'Verma's tragic vision'.

Apart from the names of the cities which repetitively appear in
he poems, almost as incantations, the poetic persona at multiple
aces is seen asking for directions or giving them. One of the
y lines – 'Horseman, / where does this road go?' – is telling of
he place-oriented approach in some poems. The binary of 'here'
nd 'there' seems necessary for establishing any kind of personal
entity, not only in *Magadh* but also in a world which is sharply
vided between the city and the countryside. The geographical
sertion, or its need, in the poems explicates the finality of this
vide. Verma himself, as we saw earlier with 'Nameless in Avanti',
as tackling issues of alienation in Delhi with an eye on his small-
wn upbringing. The dialectics of 'here' and 'there' also extend to

131

the political choices that Verma offers us in his poem 'The Thi
Way', where the first two options – 'we can act unethically / an
keep / debating ethics' and 'Speak untruth / practise untrut
while we 'wage wars for truth' – give way to a third one:

> Friends,
> there's also
> > a third way –
>
> but
> > it doesn't go
> > through
> > > Magadh,
> > > > Avanti
> > > > > Kosal
> > > > or
> > > > > Vidarbha.

The third way, exhausting all previous available routes and the
polarities, does not name a geographical site, a mode of trav
or a new ethic of walking. It does not announce its nature
contour. One is not even sure if this third way, presented almo
as a chimera here, is achievable in any real terms. *Magadh*, mu
of whose solemn geography is limited by history, politics an
in more subtle terms, humanity, makes room here for a prec
ious, impossible space that remains outside any cartograph
dictation and sensory knowledge.

MANTRA MUK
[First published in the *New Union* in 20

ACKNOWLEDGEMENTS

everyone, without whose help, comments, suggestions, excite-
ment, efforts and encouragement, this volume would not exist –
   People: Sohini Basak, Ashutosh Bhardwaj, Kanishka Gupta,
Giriraj Kiradoo, Arvind Krishna Mehrotra, Sharmistha Mohanty,
Tantra Mukim, Karthika Naïr, Vivek Narayanan, Janice Pariat,
Lisa von Randow, Arshia Sattar, Stefan Tobler, Ashok Vajpeyi,
Abhishek Verma and Anca Verma, and all the many others who
have left their mark on these pages.
   Institutions: the British Centre for Literary Translation, the
Charles Wallace India Trust, the Jamun, Nrityagram, Sangam
House and the University of East Anglia for time and space.
   Publications: *Almost Island* and *Asymptote*, where early ver-
sions of these poems appeared; Almost Island Books, for the
first edition, Westland Books and Eka, for the new Indian
edition, And Other Stories for the UK edition.
   Family and friends: for steadfastness, for being there.

RAHUL SONI

THIS BOOK WAS MADE POSSIBLE
THANKS TO THE SUPPORT OF

ron McEnery
ron Schneider
igail Walton
lam Lenson
lam Murphy
lam Paul
ris Lorenzato
ay Sharma
asdair Cross
bert Puente
ena Callaghan
ex Binks
ex Fleming
ex Johnstone
ex (Anna) Turner
exandra German
exandra Stewart
exandra Tammaro
Ersahin
Smith
Usman
ce Carrick-Smith
ce Wilkinson
an & Mo Tennant
ssa Rinaldi
ado Floresca
aia Gabantxo
alia Gomoiu
anda Milanetti
anda
ber Casiot
ber Da
elia Dowe
itav Hajra
os Hintermann
y Hatch
y Lloyd

Amy Raphael
Amy Schoffelen
Amy Sousa
Amy Tabb
Ana Novak
Anastasia Sukhanov
Andrea Barlien
Andrea Larsen
Andrea Lucard
Andrea Oyarzabal
   Koppes
Andreas Zbinden
Andrew Burns
Andrew Marston
Andrew Martino
Andrew McCallum
Andrew Milam
Andrew Place
Andrew Reece
Andrew Wright
Angela Erickson
Anna French
Anna Holmes
Anna Kornilova
Anna Milsom
Anne Buchanan Weiss
Anne Edyvean
Anne Germanacos
Anne-Marie Renshaw
Anne Ryden
Anne Willborn
Annette Hamilton
Annie McDermott
Anonymous
Ant Cotton
Anthea Parker
Anthony Brown

Anthony Fortenberry
April Woodward
Archie Davies
Aron Trauring
Asako Serizawa
Audrey Holmes
Audrey Morris
Audrey Small
Barb Turk
Barbara Mellor
Barbara Spicer
Barbora Kraml
Beatriz Brown
Becky Matthewson
Ben Dutton
Ben Peterson
Ben Schofield
Ben Thornton
Ben Walter
Ben Warren
Ben Wasson
Benjamin Heanue
Benjamin Oliver
Benjamin Pester
Beth Heim de Bera
Bill Fletcher
Billy Ray Belcourt
Blazej Jedras
Brandon Clar
Brekan Blakeslee
Brett Parker
Briallen Hopper
Brian Anderson
Brian Isabelle
Brian Smith
Bridget Ingle
Briony Hey

Brittany Redgate
Brooks Williams
Buck Johnston &
  Camp Bosworth
Burkhard Fehsenfeld
Buzz Poole
Caitlin Halpern
Caleb Bedford
Cameron Adams
Cameron Johnson
Carmen Smith
Carol Murashige
Carole Parkhouse
Carolina Pineiro
Caroline Montanari
Caroline Musgrove
Caroline West
Carrie Brogoitti
Catharine Braithwaite
Catherine Tandy
Cathryn Siegal-
  Bergman
Cecilia Rossi
Cecilia Uribe
Cerileigh Guichelaar
Chanel Martins
Charles Fernyhough
Charles Heiner
Charles Rowe
Charlie Small
Charlotte Coulthard
Charlotte Whittle
Chelsey Blankenship
Cherilyn Elston
China Miéville
Chloe Rushby
Chloe Wieland
Chris Blackmore
Chris Brook
Chris Clamp
Chris Johnstone

Chris McCann
Chris Potts
Chris Senior
Chris Stevenson
Christine Bartels
Christopher Chambers
Christopher Fox
Christopher Lin
Christopher Scott
Christopher Stout
Ciara Callaghan
Ciara Windsor
Claire Brooksby
Claire Mackintosh
Clare Burgess
Clare Young
Clare Wilkins
Claudia Mazzoncini
Clem Edwards
Cliona Quigley
Colin Denyer
Colin Matthews
Collin Brooke
Cormac O'Callaghan
Courtney Lilly
Courtney Sanford
Craig Kennedy
Cynthia De La Torre
Cyrus Massoudi
Daina Chiu
Daisy Savage
Dale Wisely
Dalia Cavazos
Daniel Cossai
Daniel Hahn
Daniel Sanford
Daniel Scarah
Daniel Syrovy
Daniela Steierberg
Danielle Moylan
Darren Boyling

Darren Gillen
Darryll Rogers
Darya Lisouskaya
Dave Appleby
Dave Lander
David Anderson
David Eales
David Gould
David Greenlaw
David Hebblethwaite
David Higgins
David Johnson-Davi
David Morris
David Shriver
David Smith
David Wacks
Deb Unferth
Deborah Gardner
Debra Manskey
Denis Larose
Denis Stillewagt &
  Anca Fronescu
Derek Golden
Devon Lane
Diane Hamilton
Diarmuid Hickey
Dillan Stenson
Dinesh Prasad
Domenica Devine
Dominic Bailey
Dominic Nolan
Dominick Santa
  Cattarina
Dominique Brocard
Dominique Hudson
Doris Duhennois
Dr Margey Kates
Dugald Mackie
Duncan Chambers
Duncan Clubb
Dyanne Prinsen

Jane Rogers
Janis Carpenter
Jason Montano
Jason Sim
Jason Timermanis
Javier Bilbatua
Jean Dubail
Jeff Brothers
Jeff Collins
Jeff Worsham
Jeffery Huang
Jen Hardwicke
Jennifer Barizo
Jennifer Fain
Jennifer Gordon
Jennifer Rothschild
Jennifer Sarha
Jennifer Yanoschak
Jenny Huth
Jeremy Sabol
Jeremy Koenig
Jess Decamps
Jess Hannar
Jess Wood
Jessica Harkins
Jessica Queree
Jessica Weetch
Jessie Lethaby
Jethro Soutar
Jill Harrison
Jo Heinrich
Jo Lateu
Joachim Magens
Joanna Luloff
Joanna Trachtenberg
Joanna Bibby-Scullion
Joao Pedro Bragatti
   Winckler
Jodie Adams
Joe Aguilar
Joe Edwardes-Evans

Joelle Young
Johannah May Black
Johannes Menzel
John Betteridge
John Carnahan
John Conway
John Gent
John Hodgson
John Miller
John Purser
John Reid
John Selby
John Shaw
John Steigerwald
John Walsh
John Whiteside
John Winkelman
John Wyatt
Jon McGregor
Jon Riches
Jonah Benton
Jonathan Blaney
Jonathan Busser
Jonathan Jefferson
Jonathan Paterson
Jonny Kiehlmann
Joseph Camilleri
Joseph Thomas
Joshua Cooper
Joshua Davis
JP Anderson
Julia Rochester
Júlia Révay
Julie Atherton
Juliet Willsher
Junius Hoffman
Jupiter Jones
Juraj Janik
Justine Sherwood
K. Lorraine Kiidumae
Kaarina Hollo

Kaktus Leach
Kalina Rose
Kara Harris
Karen Gilbert
Karen Mahinski
Kari Rodgers
Karina Cicero
Karl Kleinknecht &
   Monika Motylinska
Kat Brealey
Katarzyna
   Bartoszynska
Kate Beswick
Kate Clark
Kate Wille
Katharine Robbins
Katherine Sotejeff-
   Wilson
Katherine Spalding
Kathryn Drabinski
Kathryn Edwards
Kathryn Williams
Kathy Mitchell
Katie Freeman
Katie Zegar
Kay Caldwell
Keir Chetham
Keith Walker
Kelly Hydrick
Kenneth Blythe
Keno Jüchems
Kent McKernan
Kerri Marusiak
Kerrie Henderson
Kieran Rollin
Kieron James
Kimberlyn Pepe
Kirsten Benites
Kris Ann Trimis
Kris Fernandez-Eve
Kristen Tracey

istin Glenn
ystine Phelps
rt Navratil
le Pienaar
na Selby
ara Jakobsson
ara Ling
ara Zlatos
aren Latulip
aren Trestler
arence Laluyaux
th Binns
la Brittenham
Harbour
gh Vorhies
ona Iosifidou
vis Boyd
m Buell
ana Lobato
e Weaver
da Jones
den Franz
dsay Attree
dsey Harbour
a Adler
a Hess
a McLeman
u Tanase
Clifford
Rice & Max Spitz
na Bleach
raine Cushnie
is Lewarne
ise Evans
ise Jolliffe
isa Liljegren
inda Smith
se von Flotow
Cesar Peres
e Gaillet
e Healey

Luke Murphy
Lydia Syson
Lyndia Thomas
Lynn Fung
Lynn Martin
Lynn Grant
Mack McKenna
Madalyn Marcus
Maggie Humm
Maggie Livesey
Mairead Beeson
Maja Luna
Maree Thomas
Margaret Dillow
Maria Bardales
Marian Zelman
Mariann Wang
Marijana Rimac
Marina Castledine
Mark Reynolds
Mark Sargent
Mark Sheets
Mark Sztyber
Mark Troop
Mark Waters
Marlene Gray
Marten van der Meulen
Martin Ewing
Martin Eric Rodgers
Martin Rathgeber
Mary Clarke
Mary Tinebinal
Mary Ann Dulcich
Matt Davies
Matthew Clarke-
    Venters
Matthew Cooke
Matthew Crawford
Matthew Eatough
Matthew James Francis
Matthew Lowe

Matthew Woodman
Matthias Rosenberg
Max Gordon
Maxwell Mankoff
McKenzie MacDonald
Meaghan Delahunt
Meeka Charles
Meg Lovelock
Mel Pryor
Melissa Quignon-
    Finch
Merijn Douwes
Michael Aguilar
Michael Bichko
Michael Boog
Michael Burdett
Michael Farren
Michael Gavin
Michael Parsons
Michael James
    Eastwood
Michaela Anchan
Michelle Mirabella
Mike Abram
Mike Barrie
Mike James
Mike Schneider
Mikey Brothers
Miles Smith-Morris
Mim Lucy
Mohamed Tonsy
Molly Schneider
Mona Arshi
Monica Becerra
Morayma Jimenez
Moriah Haefner
Myla Lloyd
Myza Gouthro
Nancy Chen
Nancy Jacobson
Nancy Oakes

Naomi Morauf
Natalie Jones
Natalie Shpringman
Nathalia Robbins-
  Cherry
Nathan Weida
Nick Cain
Nick James
Nick Jowett
Nick Marshall
Nick Sidwell
Nick Slessor
Nick Twemlow
Nicolas Granger
Nicole Matteini
Niki Sammut
Nina Aron
Norman Batchelor
Odilia Corneth
Ohan Hominis
Owen Burke
Pankaj Mishra
Pankhuri Sahare
Pat Winslow
Patricia Schirmer
Patrick Hawley
Patrick Hoare
Patrick Liptak
Patrick Pagni
Paul Bangert
Paul Cray
Paul Ewing
Paul Jones
Paul Jordan
Paul Milhofer
Paul Munday
Paul Nightingale
Paul Scott
Pavlos Stavropoulos
Pearl Pandya
Pedro Ponce

Penelope Hewett
  Brown
Penny Hodgkinson
Perry Ismangil
Pete Clough
Pete Keeley
Peter Boothe
Peter Edwards
Peter Goulborn
Peter Wells
Petra Hendrickson
Philip Herbert
Philip Leichauer
Philip Warren
Phillipa Clements
Phoebe McKenzie
Phoebe Millerwhite
Phyllis Reeve
Piet Van Bockstal
Rachael de Moravia
Rachael Williams
Rachel Beddow
Rachel Belt
Rachel Coburn
Rachel Martinez
Rachel Rothe
Rachel Van Riel
Rahul Kanakia
Rajni Aldridge
Ralph Jacobowitz
Rebecca Caldwell
Rebecca Jackson
Rebecca Milne
Rebecca Moss
Rebecca Peer
Rebecca Proskauer
Rebecca Rushforth
Rebecca Servadio
Rebecca Shaak
Rebekah Lattin-
  Rawstrone

Reena Khandpur
Renee Thomas
Rhea Pokorny
Richard Corley
Richard Ellis
Richard Hughes
Richard Mansell
Richard Smith
Richard Soundy
Richard Stubbings
Richard Village
Ricka Kohnstamm
Riley Faulds
Risheeta Joshi
Rishi Dastidar
Rita Kaar
Rita Marrinson
Rita O'Brien
Robbie Matlock
Robert Gillett
Robert Selcov
Robin McLean
Robin Taylor
Robina Frank
Ronan O'Shea
Rory Williamson
Rosanna Foster
Rosemary Horsewoo
Rosie Ware
Ross Beaton
Roz Simpson
Ruth Curry
Ryan Bestford
Ryan Day
Ryan Pierce
Sabine Griffiths
Saidy Bober
Sally Ayhan
Sally Baker
Sam Ramsay
Samuel Wright

a Kittleson
a Patenaude
ah Arboleda
ah Arkle
ah Brewster
ah Carr
ah Geere
ah Jones
ah Lucas
ah Stevns
na Dugdale
tt Adams
tt Baxter
tt Chiddister
a Carswell
a Johnston
a McGivern
na Guinness
non Knapp
con Levy
ill Tippins
chi Saraswat
a Shrinath
na Kang
ak Ali
on Clark
on Robertson
one Dozier
Grout
y Rodgers
no Mula
han Eggum
hanie Miller
hanie Powell
hanie Smee

Stephanie Wasek
Stephen Fuller
Stephen Yates
Stephen Garrity
Steve Dearden
Steven Diggin
Steven Hess
Steven Norton
Stewart Eastham
Stuart Allen
Stuart Wilkinson
Suman Kumar
Summer Migliori Soto
Susan Dery
Susan Jaken
Susan Morgan
Susan Winter
Susan Wachowski
Suzanne Kirkham
Taha Belal
Takamitsu Yamamoto
Tara Roman
Tatjana Soli
Tatyana Reshetnik
Taylor Ball
Ted Franco
Terry Bone
Tess Lewis
Theresa Kelsay
Thomas Counsell
Thomas Fritz
Thomas Noone
Thomas van den Bout
Tiffany Lehr
Tim Hosgood

Timothy Baker
Toby Ryan
Tom Darby
Tom Franklin
Tom Gray
Tom Stafford
Tom Whatmore
Trevor Latimer
Trevor Wald
Trevor Brent & Marta
  Berto
Tricia Durdey
Tyler Giesen
Tyler Graber
Valerie Kulpit
Vandana Thirumale
Vanessa Baird
Vanessa Dodd
Vanessa Heggie
Vanessa Rush
Victor Meadowcroft
Vijay Pattisapu
Wendy Langridge
Weronika Aleksander
William
  Brockenborough
William Mackenzie
William Richard
William Wilson
Yoora Yi Tenen
Yort Jansen
Zachary Maricondia &
  Celia Kitchell
Zahra Al Khudairi
Zoe Taylor